STANLEY GIBBONS GUIDES

COINS OF ROMAN BRITAIN

David Miller

STANLEY GIBBONS PUBLICATIONS LTD

391 Strand, London WC2R 0LX

By Appointment to Her Majesty The Queen
Stanley Gibbons Ltd, Philatelists

© Stanley Gibbons Publications Ltd 1976

First published 1976

ISBN 0 85259 845 9

Collecting the Coins of Roman Britain

For 400 years the Romans occupied this island. Today, wherever we go, their influence remains. Our roads overlay earlier Roman ones while most major towns have Roman origins. Even on our coins Britannia, herself a Roman personification, harkens back to those issues

Gold aureus of Julius Caesar. Struck in Rome B.C.

which were struck to commemorate victories in the Roman province. Perhaps one of the most rewarding ways of studying the history of the Romans in this island is through their coinage. Coins were struck here for only fifty of the 400 years of occupation, but these coins, mainly from London, are found in huge quantities, and can be bought for a pound or so dependent on their condition. A collection of coins of Roman Britain does not have to be made up only of those coins struck here. Every advance the Romans made in this country from the invasion of A.D. 43 to the northernmost conquest of Scotland in A.D. 143 is chronicled on the coinage. Some of these coins are rare and valuable, but an example of other coins of the emperor who issued them will be only a few pounds. Some emperors who visited Britain preferred not to commemorate the fact but the table at the back of the book will help the collector not to miss any of these.

Further information can be obtained from your local museum, where displays of Roman coins can normally be seen. (For a list of some of the more notable museums the reader is referred to page 30.) The largest collection is at the British Museum where, in their new coin gallery,

Nero A.D. 54–68. Bronze dupondius. With mark of value π, meaning two asses. Found in north Lincolnshire.

Maximianus A.D. 286–310. Bronze follis.

virtually all the coins mentioned in this book can be seen, including the unique medallions of Carausius struck in Britain. Unfortunately the only medallion showing Roman London, struck around 297, is at Arras in Northern France, where it was found in 1922.

Finally, it is a good maxim to collect coins in the best condition that you can afford. On a poor specimen one can miss so much of the inscription and design that shows up on the better specimens. Most coin dealers will be pleased to help you with information on coins and aid you in your collecting. I hope that this short book will stimulate interest in a series which has so much history and scope for the new collector.

DAVID MILLER

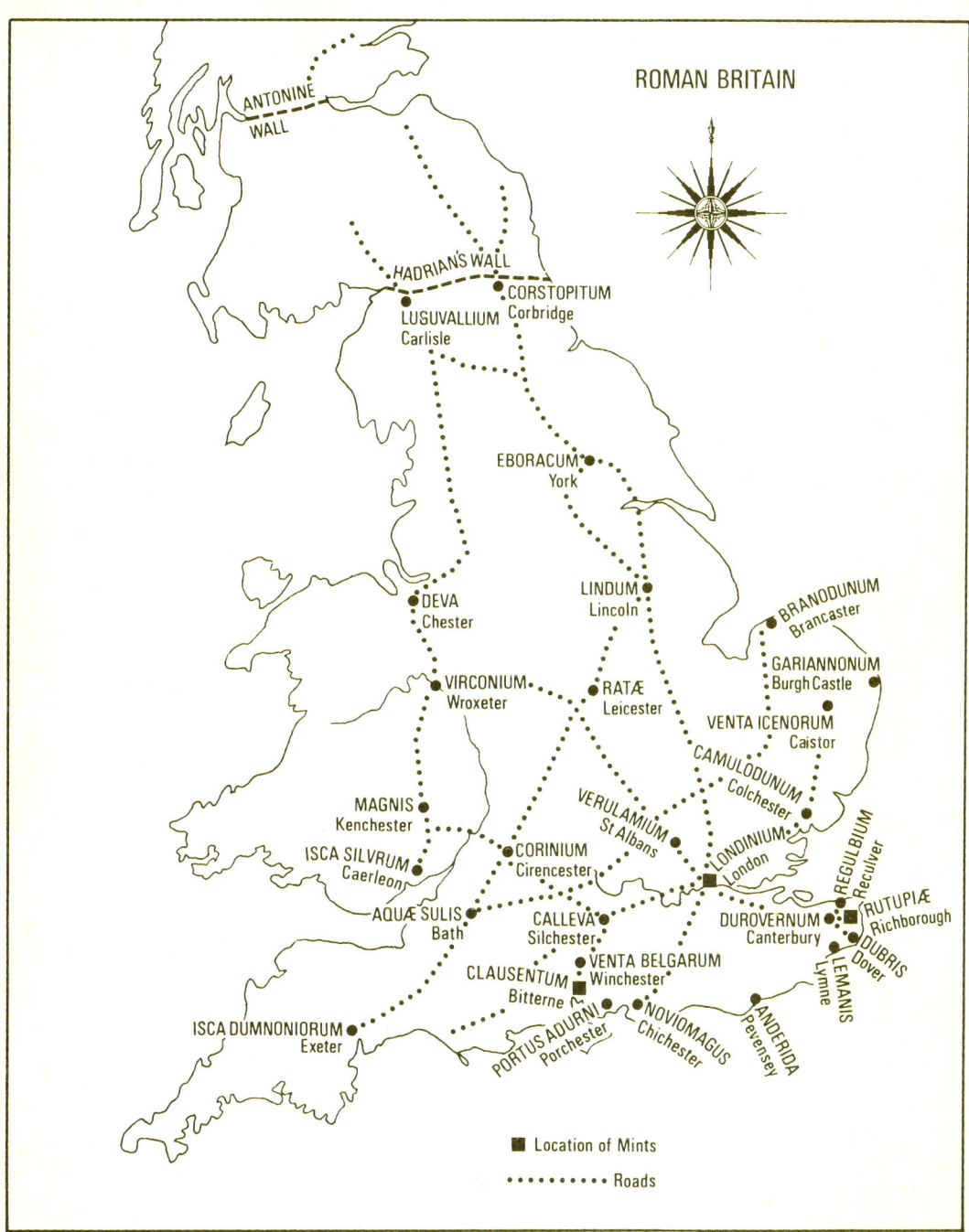

Note on Illustrations

With the exception of the chart on page 8, the coins in this publication have been reproduced at twice actual size. Those in the chart are depicted at the same size as the originals.

Roman Britain and its Coins

On a spring day in A.D. 43 the combined forces of the Roman Empire went ashore on the coast of Kent. Four legions, the second, ninth, fourteenth and twentieth, under the command of General Aulius Plautius made camp at Richborough unopposed but within a few days they were to face the armies of Britain. The British leaders Caractacus and Togodummus were defeated near Rochester and the way was clear for the invading armies to force the Thames and march on the tribal capital at Colchester.

The fall of Colchester was not, however, the fall of Britain and nearly thirty years were to pass before the Romans were to subdue their latest acquisition to the Roman Empire. The fall of Colchester was enough of a victory for the emperor Claudius to join his troops on foreign soil and thus to qualify for a triumph or victory march as victorious commander-in-chief in the field. After a few days the emperor had had enough of his new province and returned to Rome. Coins celebrating his victory were subsequently struck in gold and silver. A gold aureus and a silver denarius struck at Rome in A.D. 43 show the emperor's head on the obverse and the triumphal arch built for the victory on the reverse. Across the arch is emblazoned DE BRITANN. Even at Caesarea in Cappadocia, the other end of the Mediterranean in modern Turkey, a special issue of silver two drachms was struck showing Claudius in his triumphal chariot above the words DE BRITANNIS.

In a numismatic history of Roman Britain these coins of Claudius may not be strictly the first Roman coins of Britain. For years Roman coins had been in circulation in Britain brought by trade from the Continent while the Celtic chieftains hired Roman die-makers to design and produce their coinage or copied those of their neighbours across the Channel. Cunobelin, the greatest chieftain of this period, who ruled between A.D. 10 and A.D. 40 in the area which is now Suffolk, Berkshire, Essex and Hertfordshire,

Gold stater of Cunobelin, King of the Catuvellauni. Struck at Colchester A.D. 10–40.

Claudius A.D. 41–54. Provincial silver di-drachm struck at Caesarea, Cappadocia, now in Turkey.

ROMAN CURRENCY SYSTEM

 =

1 Gold Aureus = 25 Silver Denarii

 =

1 Silver Denarius = 4 Bronze Sestertii

 =

1 Bronze Sestertius = 2 Dupondii

 =

1 Dupondius = 2 Asses

struck coins based on the silver denarii of Augustus and those of the earlier Roman Republic. From the evidence of coin hoards it is clear that Roman coins circulated alongside the gold and silver issues of the various tribes.

As the Roman invaders advanced into Britain, so larger and larger areas came under direct Roman rule. Behind the soldiers came the traders and administrators and with them the coins of Rome. At first not enough seem to have been available perhaps because the local British coinage was melted down and sent to Rome as loot. Whatever the reason, copies or forgeries of bronze Roman coins appeared. Some of these could have been struck in travelling mints by the army for local payment before more official coins were available, or they may just have been struck by local people to augment the lack of currency. These coins, often described as Celtic copies of Claudius, are truly the first coins of Roman Britain.

The Roman monetary system at this time was made up of gold, silver and bronze coins. The gold aureus, about the size of a modern penny, was equal to twenty-five silver denarii. A denarius is often translated in the Bible and other early works as a penny, thus the tribute penny, and was worth four large bronze sestertii. This bronze issue was itself divided into smaller denominations of two dupondii or four asses, the as being worth one-sixteenth of the silver denarius. This coinage which had come into regular use under the emperor Augustus about 20 B.C. was to last until reformed in A.D. 214 by Caracalla, an emperor of whom we shall hear more later.

In Britain the armies of Rome continued to move northward and westward. Certain kings allied themselves with the newcomers and saved themselves and their territories for a short time. In the west, General Vespasian's second legion advanced on the great hill fort of the Durotriges tribe in Dorset. Mai-Dun or Maiden Castle fell after a heavy fight and the graves of the defenders show terrible injuries caused by the iron bolts of the legion's catapults. Vespasian – who in his biography tells us that in Britain he fought thirty battles, conquered two tribes, captured over twenty fortresses

Vespasian A.D. 69–79. Bronze dupondius found in Lincolnshire.

Hadrian A.D. 117–138. Bronze sestertius showing Salus, the goddess of health and safety.

and annexed the Isle of Wight – was later transferred to Palestine. Leaving, in A.D. 69, his son Titus to capture Jerusalem from the Jewish defenders he set sail to become one of the best Roman emperors after the suicide of Nero. The Colosseum, built on his orders by Jewish prisoners of war, is perhaps one of the greatest memorials of all times to a man who was proud to have annexed the Isle of Wight and helped to pacify the island of Britain.

In A.D. 61, Boudicca, Queen of the Iceni, rose up against Roman aggression. Storming down from her Norfolk capital she destroyed the Roman settlements at St. Albans, Colchester and London. It took months for the Roman army to restore order and up to 100,000 people lost their lives. Perhaps because it was such a disaster no coins were issued for this victory and Britain does not appear on Roman coins again until Hadrian visited the province in about A.D. 122.

A grave military disaster seems to have overtaken the Roman army in the north of Britain in about A.D. 118. The frontier of Roman Britain had now been moved to central Scotland, but York, founded in A.D. 73, was still the main military headquarters. Now an uprising swept away the northern command. The ninth legion stationed at York disappears from history, being probably wiped out. Hadrian decided to come and personally supervise the recovery of the province. The result was the fortified frontier which we call Hadrian's Wall. To celebrate this great victory a whole series of coins were struck, and an as struck in Rome in A.D. 120–122 shows for the first time the goddess of Britain, Britannia. She is seated facing, foot on a pile of stones, resting her head on her right hand and holding a sceptre in her left. Next to her on the right is a large shield. It has been suggested that the stones represent Hadrian's Wall but as this can hardly have been planned, let alone built, at this date it seems unlikely. In A.D. 134–138 another series of coins, a sestertius, a dupondius and an as, were again struck showing Britannia but these fall into a general series commemorating the provinces of the empire. Much rarer is another series of the same time com-

Hadrian A.D. 117–138. Bronze as. The first coin to show Britannia and commemorating Hadrian's visit to Britain.

Hadrian A.D. 117–138. Silver denarius of the Rome mint.

Antoninus Pius A.D. 138–161. Bronze sestertius. Britannia appears now more as we know her.

memorating Hadrian's visit to Britain and the army of the province. The first type with the legend ADVENTVI AVG BRITANNIAE shows the emperor sacrificing at an altar with a female figure, probably Britannia, watching him.

The first series shows Hadrian on horseback being greeted by standard bearers of the army in Britain. Another type shows him actually addressing his soldiers from a saluting base. Coins of the Britannia type can be bought occasionally, the as from around £30, but the military series are only known from a very few specimens.

Despite the success of Hadrian's frontier policy it was decided that the tribes of the north beyond the Wall needed further subjugation. Consequently around A.D. 140 the Romans again advanced north and built a new barrier known as the Antonine Wall between the Forth and the Clyde. It consisted of

Antoninus Pius A.D. 138–161. Bronze sestertius struck at Rome to commemorate the British victories.

Antoninus Pius. Bronze sestertius. A victory flying left holding a laurel wreath proclaims the victory of Rome in Britain.

nineteen forts joined by a turf wall and protected by a deep ditch in front. Units were brought up from Hadrian's Wall and the south to man the frontier. In Rome it was decided that this further expansion of the British province merited a new victory issue. (It should be said at this point that the Roman coinage not only had a monetary use but was the medium of mass propaganda. We will see later how other emperors used this with varying success.) Thus the advisers of the new emperor, Antoninus Pius, decided that the British victory should be widely acclaimed and the populace duly informed. All denominations in all metals were used and the series began sometime in A.D. 140 and carried on for four years. Most coins show Britannia seated on a rock, holding a military standard and spear and leaning on a shield. Others refer to the victory itself with a winged Victory either holding a wreath or carrying a shield with the legend BRITAN on it. A rare sestertius shows for the first time Britannia helmeted with spear and shield and of similar design to the present type on modern coins.

Antoninus Pius. Bronze as. This is the most common of the Britannia series and is often found on Roman sites in England.

In A.D. 155 the Brigantes, a tribe covering most of north-east Britain, once more revolted and overran the few garrisons left in their area. Military installations on both Hadrian's Wall and the Antonine Wall show signs of destruction. Reasons for the tribal uprising are unknown but the Roman victory was deemed great enough for another issue of coins from Rome, this time showing a Britannia in a more subdued mood, her head on her right hand, with her shield and standard resting behind her. This issue of coins was only in the sestertius and the as but they are the commonest of Britannia coins. The asses are often of bad style and it is possible that many were struck officially or unofficially in Britain itself. These coins are mostly found in poor condition which argues that they were in circulation for a long time or that the production of them was not of the highest quality.

For the next twenty-five years the north of Britain remained unsettled but in March 180 the tribes of central Scotland overran the two great Walls and invaded the province. Such was the force of this attack that it appears to have taken the Roman government four years to bring the situation under control. By A.D. 184 the province was no longer under threat though the Antonine Wall and the area behind it had fallen for ever to the barbarians. Now Hadrian's Wall, restored and refortified, was the northern-most limit of the Roman Empire. The government of the emperor Commodus produced a large issue of bronze sestertii showing a Victory seated above the legend VICT BRIT. Medallions were struck and even the emperor's Egyptian subjects were informed of the success through the local issues of tetradrachms at Alexandria. Here Commodus was shown beside prisoners above the Greek legend BOETANNI. Commodus for all his talk of victories was not popular. His favourites ran the government while he became distinctly mad. He believed that he was the reincarnation of Hercules and demanded that he be worshipped as a god. On his coins he appears dressed in the lion's skin head-dress of the deity. This was too much even for a people used to the extremes of their rulers. On the last day of the year A.D. 192 the praetorian prefect, the head of the emperor's guard and his court chamberlain acted. The emperor was throttled by a professional wrestler as he was taking his bath and for the first time since the death of Nero in

Septimius Severus A.D. 193–211. Bronze sestertius.

A.D. 68 the empire was without a legitimate ruler.

A new ruler was hurriedly appointed in Rome by the Senate but Pertinax was unable to gain the confidence of the people and he was murdered by the army after a reign of only eighty-six days. The praetorian guards having deposed two emperors in succession announced that the job would now go to the highest bidder. M. Didius Julianus offered 25,000 sestertii a man or 250 gold aurei. As the aureus was about the same weight as a gold sovereign this means in modern terms that each soldier got about £6,500. Such was the indignation in Rome over these circumstances that the populace appealed to the governor of Syria to come to their aid. However, two other governors saw their chance to gain the purple and prepared to advance on Rome.

The governors in question were Clodius Albinus, governor of Britain, and Septimius Severus, governor of Upper Pannonia, now modern Hungary. Severus advanced on Rome first having made a deal with Albinus. His troops had already proclaimed him emperor though Didius Julianus still lived. In order to protect his flank Severus created Albinus Caesar or heir-apparent. As his army arrived at the walls of Rome Julianus, who had reigned only sixty-six days, was beheaded by his own followers. Severus now controlled the capital and left for the east to deal with the governor of Syria, Pescennius Niger. The latter had also been proclaimed emperor by his soldiers but was defeated and executed by Severus in A.D. 194. Now Severus turned back to the west. In the following year he had Albinus declared a public enemy and the governor of Britain took the only option open to him and proclaimed himself rival emperor to Severus. Troops from all over Britain were moved south and preparations made for shipping them to Gaul. As Albinus's army moved south so Severus's came north. On 19 February 197 the two armies met at Lugdunum, modern Lyons, in central France. In order to pay his British troops Albinus had had silver denarii struck showing clasped hands holding a legionary eagle. The legend FIDES LEGION

COS II, referred in vain to his faith in his legions. They were defeated. Albinus was captured and along with his family executed and the bodies thrown into the Rhone. His paymaster's fate is unknown but the nice new denarii struck to pay his troops were hidden and only found in modern times. Thus most of the coins of Albinus as emperor are in virtually mint state while the coins of him as Caesar are found in almost every condition of wear.

Severus was now sole ruler of the Empire. His political and military opponents were dead but one major disaster marred his victory. Britain, denuded of troops by Albinus, was once again invaded by the barbarians from the north. In A.D. 197 Hadrian's Wall was overrun and the northern part of the island occupied. Severus dispatched a new governor-general and fresh troops to recover the province. The barbarians were rolled back and the Wall repaired. Such is the folk memory of this that, for many hundreds of years afterwards, Severus rather than Hadrian was credited with the building of the Wall.

The emperor decided that the peace of the province was unlikely while the barbarians posed a threat in Scotland. Consequently the entire imperial family, the emperor, his wife Julia Domna and his two sons, Caracalla and Geta, arrived in Britain in A.D. 208. Advancing north of Hadrian's Wall Severus's troops subdued the tribe and in 210 the Rome mint announced the new victory VICTORIAE BRIT., Victory in Britain, on the coins. Once again all denominations were pressed into service. Victories holding spears and shields in various poses pro-

Julia Domna. Provincial bronze of Antioch in Syria.

claimed the prowess of Roman arms against the enemies of the empire. Both Caracalla and Geta received the title BRITANNICVS or victors in Britain and this duly appeared on all coins of the empire. Severus meanwhile was ailing. Already in 198 he had made his elder son Caracalla joint-emperor and by 209 the younger son had also been granted the purple. Severus hoped for joint rulers to take over smoothly after his death. But

Reverse of bronze sestertius of Caracalla. Two victories erecting military trophy commemorate the British victory of Caracalla and Septimius Severus.

Geta as Caesar. Silver denarius. Struck in Rome during his father's reign.

on 4 February 211, worn out by continuing campaigning in Caledonia, he died and was cremated at the military capital of York. Geta, who was governor-general of Britain, and his elder brother and joint-emperor Caracalla presided over the funerary rites. Within weeks the two new emperors left for Rome carrying the ashes of their late father to be placed in a suitable mausoleum in the capital. Within a year Geta was to be assassinated on his brother's orders.

For seven more years Caracalla was to remain emperor and then in 217 he was also murdered. His death and the subsequent upheaval had little effect on Britain. Emperors came and went and even the thousandth anniversary of Rome in 248 caused no particular upheaval in the province. For the next thirty years the empire was never at peace. Between A.D. 248 and A.D. 284 there were over thirty major claimants to the throne. At one time the provinces of the west split away from the empire and set up their own administration. It is probable that under the emperor Postumus (A.D. 259–268) the provinces of Gaul, Spain and Britain declared their independence. From coin evidence it is certain that Britain was supplied mainly with the coinage of the Gallic usurpers. Postumus's successors continued to hold their independence until A.D. 273. By this time coinage in Britain was becoming scarce and local copies of the coinage of Tetricus (270–273) came into circulation. Most Roman sites in Britain produce these coins which have been named 'barbarous radiates' from the style and from the radiate crowns on the heads of the emperors shown.

During the reign of Caracalla new currency reforms had been evolved. The denarius, the main silver coin until this time, had at the end of A.D. 214 been partially superseded by the antoninianus of double value. This two-denarii piece gradually took over as the main coin of the empire. The old bronze coinage gradually became defunct as raging inflation due to the civil wars and collapse of the economy grew worse. By the mid-260s silver coins

Diocletian A.D. 284–305. Bronze follis of Siscia, showing the genius, or spirit, of the Roman people.

had almost disappeared and the antoninianus had now become a bronze-looking coin with only a minute portion of silver to its name. The coins got more and more erratic in shape and weight and in Britain in particular large quantities of locally produced money came into circulation. In A.D. 284 Diocletian, commander of the imperial bodyguard, assumed power after yet another assassination.

Diocletian, of humble parentage, by his military prowess rose high in the ranks of the Roman army until he became commander of the Emperor Numerian's bodyguard. When the emperor was murdered, he was proclaimed the new emperor by his troops and after a short period of strife his position was consolidated. Having retained the purple, he realised the impossibility of one man trying to rule an entity

Carausius A.D. 287–293. Bronze antoninianus struck at London but with no mint mark.

the size of the empire. He appointed Maximianus Herculeus, a successful general, as junior partner with responsibilities of ruling the west. One of Maximian's first jobs was to pacify Gaul, at that time in the midst of an uprising of the Bagaudae, or peasantry. This was put down and the emperor's next task was to strengthen the naval and shore defences of Brittany, north-east Gaul and Belgium which were frequently raided by foreign pirates. The man chosen to manage this task was Mausaeus Carausius, an officer who had served with distinction in the campaign against the Bagaudae. He was given command of the fleet stationed at Boulogne 'to keep all quiet at sea along the coast of Belgica and Amorica, which the Franks and Saxons infested.'

Carausius, according to the mediaeval chroniclers, notably Geoffrey of Monmouth, was of British birth. Aurelius

Maximian A.D. 286–310. Bronze follis of Aquileia in Italy. The reverse shows Moneta, the goddess of money.

Victor, a contemporary historian, tells us that he was a native of Menapia, the lowlands between the Waal and the Scheldt now occupied by southern Holland. However, the Menapiae were a seafaring and trading people and had established many merchant colonies on the coast of Britain and the admiral may have spent his boyhood in one of these. Whatever the origins of his birth, the new commander must have soon come into contact with British affairs. His naval command of the Classis Britannica, or British fleet, covered the large naval bases in the south-east of England. With his headquarters at Boulogne, he commanded Lymne, Richborough and Dover. From the lighthouse at Boulogne he could see its twin, beacon flaring, at Dover and know that all was under his control.

Piracy in the Channel had long been a problem for the Roman administration and Carausius seems to have dealt with it efficiently. However, according to various enemies, he used to capture the Saxon and Frankish ships after they had plundered the Roman merchantmen and kept the booty for himself. It was further said that he saw to it that the pirates knew the sailing times and routes of the most heavily laden and profitable ships. News of this situation reached the central government and Maximian, now raised to be equal colleague of Diocletian, gave orders for the arrest and execution of the admiral.

On hearing the news of his impending arrest, Carausius took action. It is not certain whether he had planned this course of action, more likely circumstances dictated them, but he declared

Carausius A.D. 287–293. Bronze antoninianus struck at London with mint mark MLXXI.

himself emperor and was hailed as such by his troops. Their acceptance seems to confirm his enemies' grudging remarks that he was a brave and clever general and he may have well lined the purses of the sailors and soldiers at Boulogne. On his assumption of the purple he sailed out of the harbour with the rest of the fleet, leaving a loyal garrison to defend the base. For the moment contemporary sources cease and one has to rely on the fifteenth-century Scottish chronicler, Hubert Boethius, who may have had access to earlier writings. According to Boethius, the fleet sailed down the Channel avoiding the uncertain naval bases on the British shore and arrived off the coast of Westmorland. Here Carausius is said to have allied himself with the Picts and Scots and then marched on York, the main military depot for the north of Britain and the supply base for

Allectus A.D. 293–296. Bronze antoninanus of the London mint.

the Wall. Here the troops of the governor of Britain met him in pitched battle, during which several British units refused to fight. With their withdrawal the battle was lost for the governor's army. They were defeated and their commander and his staff slain. Later in his reign Carausius issued a series of coins honouring various legions stationed within his sphere of influence. It is some confirmation of this battle that a major omission is that of the sixth legion stationed at York, which presumably fought for the central government and lost the day.

With the governor dead and the army now firmly on his side, Carausius marched for London and set up a mint to produce his new coinage. In the hurriedness of his departure he had brought few experts and no blanks with which to strike the coins. The first coins of the new reign were, therefore, restrikes over issues of previous emperors. The reverses told of peace and luck to the new province. Less lucky though were the loyal troops in Boulogne. The base had been taken by Maximian who was informed that 'already the ebb and flow of the tide has sucked in the blood of your enemies slain upon that coast.' This blood-thirsty panegyric delivered to the emperor at Trier on 21 April 289 marked the outset of the first Roman attempt to bring Britain under the central government once again. The author, Claudius Mamestinus, finishes thus, 'O, emperor, what a happy issue will attend you in your sea operation against the pirate when even the weather is at your service.' Fortunately for Carausius the Roman fleet was scattered by a storm in the Channel and the remnants defeated by the superior forces of the British fleet. As a result of this victory and because of rebellions in other parts of the empire, a temporary peace was made and a part of northern France, including Rouen and the base at Boulogne, ceded to Carausius. His claim was recognised and to celebrate the fact the Clausentum (Bitterne) mint issued a coin with the busts of Diocletian, Carausius and Maximian under the legend CARAVSIVS ET FRATRES SVI – Carausius and his brothers.

In Britain the political and economic position was improving. New coins of much higher quality were being produced and for the first time in fifty years a regular issue of silver coins was made. Three mints were now operating, London and the two naval bases of Bitterne at Southampton and Richborough in Kent. Gold, silver and bronze coins were struck

Allectus A.D. 293–296. Bronze antoninianus of the 'C' mint. Originally thought to be Colchester, this mint is now given to Bitterne.

and for at least a year Carausius continued to strike coins in the name of his continental rivals, Diocletian and Maximian. As well as this other coins of his produced reverses with PAX AVGGG, or the peace of the three emperors, as against the normal PAX AVG, the peace of only one.

In A.D. 292, Diocletian raised to the purple two new junior emperors, or Caesars. These were to take over the succession and the first job of one of them, Constantius Chlorus, was to retake the Gallic provinces of the British usurper. This he did and Boulogne fell after a short siege. In Britain Carausius's position was less tenable and in A.D. 293 he was murdered by his finance minister, Allectus. One story is that Allectus had been embezzling the exchequer and had had Carausius killed to save himself. Another possibility is that he led a group disenchanted with the loss of the continental possessions and on not getting satisfaction from the easy-going Carausius had him killed. One of the first acts of the new reign was to produce new coins. The silver coinage had not lasted long, indeed it may have only been struck for overseas trading, and now only gold and bronze remained. The new coins were of a high standard. Allectus, the civil servant, is shown mostly in military dress and continued to strike almost as many reverse types as Carausius had. The coins speak of the virtue, generosity and victory of the emperor and a new bronze coin, the quinarius, shows the emperor's main hope, a British war galley. Allectus's hope was in vain.

In A.D. 296, after many months of preparation, Constantius Chlorus had assembled two huge fleets on the coast of Gaul. These were to descend on the Bri-

Two varieties of the quinarius of Allectus struck at the naval base of Bitterne, showing British naval vessels.

tish coast in a two-pronged attack in an attempt to split the enemy's forces. The first fleet under the Caesar himself was based at Boulogne while in the mouth of the Seine, just off Le Havre, lay the second fleet under the command of the praetorian prefect, Asclepiodotus. The day for the invasion dawned and from Boulogne Constantius set sail for the Thames estuary or the north-east coast of Kent. Further south, the weather had worsened and the fleet commanders had doubts over the wisdom of setting sail. However, when news arrived of Constantius's departure the troops themselves took a hand and shouting against hesitation and delay demanded to follow Caesar whom they said had probably already arrived. The troops' impatience paid off for shortly after the fleet had sailed the weather slackened and then a thick fog descended in mid-Channel.

Just off the Isle of Wight lay the British fleet on which Allectus pinned most of his hopes. This fleet had at least once previously fought and destroyed a Roman war fleet in the Channel. Now it had to do it again. The most likely place for an invasion was between Dover and Southampton and Allectus seems to have gambled on the western end of this area

Constantius Chlorus. Bronze follis struck when Caesar, showing the genius of the Roman people.

being chosen. Here there were several good harbours and naval bases while inland the cities of Winchester and Chichester with the surrounding rich countryside would make a good base for a foraging army. The emperor knew now that the people were no longer on his side and little, if anything, would be done by the civilian population to hinder the Roman army. But the fog thickened as the two fleets approached each other. The Roman fleet, the noise of the men and oars muffled by the fog, sailed on past the opposition and made landfall at Bitterne. The British fleet, still off the Isle of Wight, remained at its station oblivious of the enemy now on the coast behind it.

Having disembarked the troops,

Constantius Chlorus. Gold aureus struck in Rome when he was Caesar.

Asclepiodotus ordered the ships to be burned. The troops had now no means of escape but this act of bravado seemed to have heartened them even more, believing as they did that the other fleet had landed and was already joining the battle. Constantius, however, with his fleet was at that moment becalmed off the north coast of Kent by the same weather as had brought up the fog in the Channel.

Word had by now reached Allectus in London of the landing at the naval base at Bitterne. Soon news came in of the second fleet lying off the coast of Kent. Realising that his position was in peril with two field armies in different parts of the country and that his fleet had failed to make any impact at all, Allectus chose to destroy the army already on the coast and trust to luck that he could reassemble his troops to combat the other army when it disembarked. Troops had been brought south many months before and now by a series of forced marches these all assembled as Allectus marched south to join battle with Asclepiodotus.

The site of this battle has never been finally established though Woolmer Common in Hampshire is the most accepted site. Here Asclepiodotus awaited the army of Allectus. According to Eumenius, a contemporary writer, on seeing the imperial troops, Allectus became panic-stricken 'and neither drew out his army in battle array nor drew up all the forces which he was hurrying with him but . . . rushed upon his doom.' The emperor had little skill as a soldier, having been a politician and financial expert, and his new advisers were not used to pitched battles, being mostly barbarian mer-

The Arras Medallion. Gold medallion struck at Trier in Germany to commemorate Constantius's victory over Allectus in A.D. 296.

cenaries. The result of this panic was a bloody rout and Allectus and his mercenaries beat a hurried retreat from the field. The emperor, now in disguise, was hunted down by the Romans and his party overwhelmed. His body, found later, was with little difficulty identified as that of the late emperor.

In the Channel Constantius's fleet, for so long becalmed, was now beating down the Thames estuary towards London. Here all was confusion as the Frankish mercenaries looted the city in the aftermath of defeat. On to this scene of destruction came the Roman fleet. The Franks hastily broke off their looting and tried to take to the war galleys moored on the Thames. They were too late. Roman troops poured into the city, hacking down any barbarians they could see. A medal commemorating this victory was found at Arras in France. It shows Constantius on horseback being received at the gates of London by the Genius of the city while on the Thames a Roman galley sails. REDDITOR LV.CIS AETERNAE reads the legend and to the people of London, after three years of misrule, the restorer of Eternal Light of Roman civilisation must have seemed a saviour. Crowds mobbed him in the streets, singing his praises and cheering whenever he appeared. They had every reason to, for it had been decided to treat the breakaway province not as one recaptured from traitors but as an area restored to Roman rule after barbarian occupation.

While Britain had gone its own way, in the main empire Diocletian had instituted some drastic monetary reforms. The antoninianus, for so long a debased bronze coin, was superseded by a new larger bronze follis. This follis was tarifed at five to the silver argenteus and 120 to the gold aureus and was worth two-and-a-half times the defunct antoninianus. Mint marks occasionally used up to this time now appear regularly on all the coins. One exception occurs. When Constantius invaded Britain he brought over the new coinage without mint marks. These may have been struck on the Continent for use in Britain if the war had been long drawn out. With the capture of London the mint started to issue the new coins.

The new coinage, the bronze follis, began production with the same type of reverse in use over the whole of the empire. The Genius of the Roman People stood holding a cornucopia, the symbol of the empire's abundance. Below him proudly was the new London mint sign of LON. This issue was to be short and for unknown, but possibly political, reasons the mint mark was dropped off subsequent issues and it was not until the summer of 307 that a new mint mark of PLN appeared. The P found on most London mint coins is short for PECUNIA, or Money. Other variants show SM or MS, an abbreviation for SACRA MONETA, or Sacred Money.

On 25 July 306 Constantius, on a visit to Britain to help repel another Pictish invasion, died at York. His son by his first wife Helena, Constantine, was proclaimed emperor by the troops and thus disrupted the carefully balanced hierarchy of the two emperors and the two Caesars. At first an attempt was made to keep the peace but within months several new contestants had come into the ring. Several rebellions occurred and the mint of London celebrated the new British ruler's political hopes by putting its new mint mark proudly on its coins. By 308 the chaos in the empire was such that a conference of all protagonists was called. Various people abdicated, some were demoted, others proscribed and in all no one was satisfied. The result was

Constantine the Great A.D. 307–337. Bronze follis of London. The reverse shows the spirit of the Roman people.

Maximinus II A.D. 309–313. Bronze follis of London. Found in north Lincolnshire.

Galerius A.D. 305–311. Bronze follis of London. Note the smaller size to the earlier type of ten years before.

further civil war.

During this period of strife the coins of London had mirrored the political upheavals. The original tetrarchy, that is the Augustus Diocletian and Maximianus I and their two junior colleagues, the Caesars Constantius and Galerius, had all appeared on identical issues from London. When the Caesars had taken over, their new junior colleagues, Severus II and Maximinus II, also appeared. But with Constantine taking power in 306 the mint no longer struck coins of his rivals. Only Licinius I – the only man to come out of the great conference with any gain – appears when he had been appointed Augustus of the West. Constantine felt able to support him and so London struck coins with his portrait.

For the next few years Constantine

Licinius I A.D. 308–324. Bronze follis of London.

Constantine the Great. Gold solidus of Nicodemia, in modern Turkey.

grabbed more and more power for himself. Rivals were removed and provinces taken over. By 313 the final rival was destroyed and the empire was now controlled by Licinius and Constantine. Licinius now kept the eastern half while Constantine controlled the west. Three new Caesars were appointed as all earlier ones were now dead. Two of these were sons of Constantine and one the son of Licinius. Crispus and Constantine II both had coins struck in London but Licinius's son, Licinius II, never appears. In A.D. 324 Constantine seized sole power. Licinius and his son were defeated in battle and though allowed to retire into private life were later executed. With control of the empire, Constantine now proceeded to reform the currency. Inflation had reduced the bronze coins in size and silver

Constantine the Great. Bronze follis of London. The reverse shows the 'Unconquered Sun-God'.

had almost completely disappeared. The new basis of the currency was a slightly lighter gold coin called the solidus. There was also a new silver coin, a siliqua, struck at twenty-four to the gold piece. The bronze coins continued to be struck at the small module to which they had been reduced due to the inflation.

In 337 Constantine died, nominally a Christian, though his London coins had continued to his death to show reverses of Mars and the Sun God. His empire was split up between his surviving sons, Constans, Constantius II and Constantine II, who promptly declared war on each other in a scramble for supremacy. In the general chaos Britain again was overrun by barbarians and the London mint, after a life of fifty years, closed down. It was never to reopen for regular work.

With no coins being made in London, the province partially overrun and the rest of the empire at war, regular coinage became scarce. Local copies of the coins of Constantius II, showing Roman soldiers spearing fallen barbarians, circulated alongside their regular counterparts. These coins were very crude and hark back to the work made during the 270s when Britain had before been cut off from the Continent. Commercial disruption was further augmented by the setting up of a rival empire in Gaul under Magnentius in 350. In 360 Britain was once again attacked by the Picts and though an army was sent from the Continent, which was now under Roman control again, it was withdrawn by Julian II to help in his revolt against Constantius II. Four years later another major attack

Constantine the Great. London follis showing the emperor on horseback.

Constantine the Great. London mint follis with reverse of Mars.

happened which was beaten off but in 368 disaster overwhelmed the province. The Picts overran Hadrian's Wall while tribes invaded from Ireland in conjunction with a Saxon attack on the east coast. The remaining legions in Britain were destroyed and only the southern towns held out behind their fortified walls. The Roman government sent help and after some time the Roman forces fought their way back to the northern frontier of Hadrian's Wall. In honour of this great victory London was renamed AUGUSTA after the emperor's title of Augustus. It is on this renaming that evidence for a final mint in London rests.

After the great victory of the Romans, one of the high-ranking officers, Magnus Maximus, had remained behind. He continued to campaign against the barbarians and probably finished up as military commander-in-chief of the province. In 383 Magnus Maximus was proclaimed emperor. Coins in gold and silver of him are found with a mint mark AVG on them. If this refers to Augusta, the contemporary name for London, then these solidi and siliquae are the last official coins of London. Magnus Maximus with his son Flavius Victor withdrew the troops from Britain and was defeated and killed. His rival was left to try and recover the province once again from the barbarians who had swept in on the news that Maximus had withdrawn his forces to Gaul. For twenty years Rome held Britain but in 410 the British troops raised another emperor Constantine III to the purple. Once again the pattern unfolded. The Roman troops left with their nominee to try their luck in Gaul against the emperor. With their departure the barbarians rushed in and the province was destroyed. In Gaul the British troops were defeated and the central government once more had to reconquer Britain – except that this time it failed. The government was too weak and under attack across the Rhine

Constantine the Great. Bronze follis of London with reverse of the Sun-God.

Constantine III A.D. 407–411. Silver siliqua of Trier with Roma seated on the reverse.

from the Goths. Some attempt was made to control the southern half of the province but gradually Britain declined economically and politically. The barbarians moved in, first as hired mercenaries and then as occupiers. The coinage declined to small pieces of scrap metal known as minims, some so small that fifty could be placed on a two-pence piece. These could only have been used to augment barter. Late Roman coins continued to be occasionally used and it was these that the Saxon conquerors copied for the designs of the first coins of England.

Major Reverse Types on British Mint Coins

Carausius (A.D. 287–293)

PAX AVG. (*Peace of the Emperor*). Pax standing left holding wreath and sceptre.

PAX AVGGG. (*Peace of the Three Emperors*). Pax standing as before. Issued after the détente with Diocletian and Maximian.

PROVIDENT(IA) AVG. Providentia (goddess of forethought) standing left holding globe and sceptre.

SALVS AVG. (*Welfare of the Emperor*). Salus standing feeding snake either in arms or on altar.

LAETITIA AVG. (*Joy or Gladness of the Emperor*). Galley with rowers or the goddess Laetitia standing holding anchor and javelin. Both types refer to Carausius's naval background.

MARTI PACIF. Mars left with olive branch, spear and shield.

Allectus (A.D. 293–296)

PAX AVG. Similar types to those of Carausius.

COMES AVG. Victory advancing right with wreath and palm.

SALVS AVG. As those of Carausius.

SPES AVG. (*Hope of the Emperor*). Spes advancing left holding up skirt and with flower in hand.

VIRTVS AVG. Galley right or left. Mostly found on the 'quinarii'.

Coins of the Tetrarchy (A.D. 296–306)

GENIO POPVLI ROMANI. Genius of the Roman people standing left holding cornucopiae and dish. This is the most common type of the period. Sometimes the legend is shortened to GENIO POP.ROM.

COMITI AVG. Sol standing left holding globe and whip.

MEMORIA FELIX. Altar between two eagles. This memorial coin was struck after the death of Constantius I in A.D. 306.

PROVIDENTIA DEORVM QVIES AVGG. Female figure standing right extending her hand to Providence standing facing her. Issued to mark the abdication of Diocletian and Maximanus.

The House of Constantine (A.D. 306–340)

ADVENTVS AVG. Emperor on horseback left with spear.

BEATA TRANQLITAS. Altar inscribed VOTIS XX surmounted by globe.

CONCORD MILITVM. (*Harmony of the Soldiers*). Concordia holding military standards.

CAESARVM NOSTRORVM. (*Our Caesar*). Wreath enclosed VOT X. Issued for the Caesars Crispus and Constantine II.

MARTI PACIF. Mars advancing left with olive branch, spear and shield.

PRINCIPI IVVENTVTIS. (*Prince of Youth*). Emperor or Caesar standing left or right with globe and spear.

PROVIDENTIAE AVGG. Gateway with towers symbolising the forethought of the Emperor in protecting the Empire.

SOLI INVICTO COMITI. (*The Unconquered Sun-God*). Sol standing left raising right hand and holding globe. The most common of Constantine's coinage.

VIRTVS EXERCIT. (*Courage of the Army*). Standard between two seated captives.

Mint Marks
Carausius and Allectus (A.D. 287–296)
London   ML–MLXXI–MSL–QL
Bitterne   C–MSCL
Richborough   RSR

Under the Tetrarchy (A.D. 296–306)
London   No mint mark–LON–PLN

Under the House of Constantine (A.D. 306–340)
London   PLN–MLL–MSL–P.LON.

Some Museums displaying Roman Coins

Aylesbury
Buckinghamshire County Museum, Church Street, Aylesbury, Buckinghamshire.

Bedford
Bedford Museum, The Embankment, Bedford, Bedfordshire.

Cambridge
Fitzwilliam Museum, Cambridge, Cambridgeshire.

Canterbury
Royal Museum, High Street, Canterbury, Kent.

Chester
Grosvenor Museum, Grosvenor Street, Chester, Cheshire.

Colchester
Colchester and Essex Museum, Colchester, Essex.

Dorchester
Dorset County Museum, High Street West, Dorchester, Dorset.

Glasgow
Hunterian Museum, Glasgow G12 8QO, Scotland.

London
British Museum, Great Russell Street, London WC1B 3DG.

Luton
Luton Museum and Art Gallery, Wardown Park, Luton, Bedfordshire LU2 7HA.

Norwich
Castle Museum, Norwich, Norfolk NR1 3JV.

Oxford
Heberden Coin Room, Ashmolean Museum, Beaumont Street, Oxford OX1 2PH.

Sheffield
Sheffield City Museum, Weston Park, Sheffield, South Yorkshire S10 2TP.

Winchester
Winchester City Museum, The Square, Winchester, Hampshire.

Further Reading

General Roman Numismatics

Coins of Greece and Rome, by R.A.G. Carson (Hutchinson).
Roman Coins, by Harold Mattingly (Methuen).
Roman Imperial Coinage (9 volumes), (Spink).
Roman Coins, by C.H.V. Sutherland (Barrie & Jenkins).
Coin Hoards (Royal Numismatic Society).
Roman Coins and their Values, by David R. Sear (B.A. Seaby).
Roman History from Coins, by Michael Grant (Cambridge University Press).

Romano–British Numismatics

The Coinage of Roman Britain, by G. Askew (B.A. Seaby).
Coins and Archaeology, by L.R. Laing (Weidenfeld & Nicolson).

Romano-British History

Roman Britain and Early England, by P.H. Blair (Nelson).
Roman Britain and the English Settlements, by Collingwood and Meyers (Oxford).
Roman Britain, by I. Richmond (Pelican History of England).
Britannia, by Shepherd Frere (Cardinal).
Britain in the Roman Empire, by Joan Liversedge (Cardinal).
Britain: Rome's Most Northerly Province, by G.M. Durant (Bell).

Romano-British Sites

A Guide to Roman & Prehistoric Monuments in England and Wales, by Jacquetta Hawkes (Cardinal).
Roman Remains in Britain, by Roger Wilson (Constable).
Seeing Roman Britain, by Leonard Cottrell (Pan).

Also available:

Many Guides to Individual Sites, published by the Department of the Environment and available from Government Book Shops.

Also Catalogues of various Museum Collections including Romano–British items from the British Museum, etc. (*See* Museum list opposite.)

Acknowledgments

I would like to thank Mr R.A.G. Carson and the Staff of the British Museum for help and information on coins of Roman Britain; my wife, Monica, for the help on the manuscript; and Mr Peter Davey for taking the photographs.

D.M.

Roman Emperors connected with Britain

A.D.		Visited Britain	Coins refer to	Coins struck in	Page
41–54	Claudius	✓	✓		7
69–79	Vespasian	✓			9
117–138	Hadrian	✓	✓		10
138–161	Antoninus Pius		✓		12
177–192	Commodus		✓		13
195–197	Clodius Albinus	✓			14
193–211	Septimius Severus	✓	✓		14
	Julia Domna, *his wife*	✓			15
198–217	Caracalla	✓	✓		15
209–212	Geta	✓	✓		15
287–293	Carausius	✓	✓	✓	17
284–305	Diocletian			✓	17
293–296	Allectus	✓		✓	20
286–310	Maximian			✓	19
305–306	Constantius I	✓	†	✓	20
305–311	Galerius			✓	24
306–307	Severus II			✓	24
309–313	Maximinus II			✓	24
308–324	Licinius I			✓	24
307–337	Constantine I	✓		✓	23
	Helena, *his mother*	?		✓	23
	Fausta, *his wife*			✓	23
317–326	Crispus, *Caesar*			✓	25
337–340	Constantine II			✓	25
337–361	Constantius II			✓	26
337–350	Constans	✓			26
383–388	Magnus Maximus	✓		?	27
387–388	Flavius Victor	?			27
407–411	Constantine III	✓			27

?=possibly   †=only on medallion